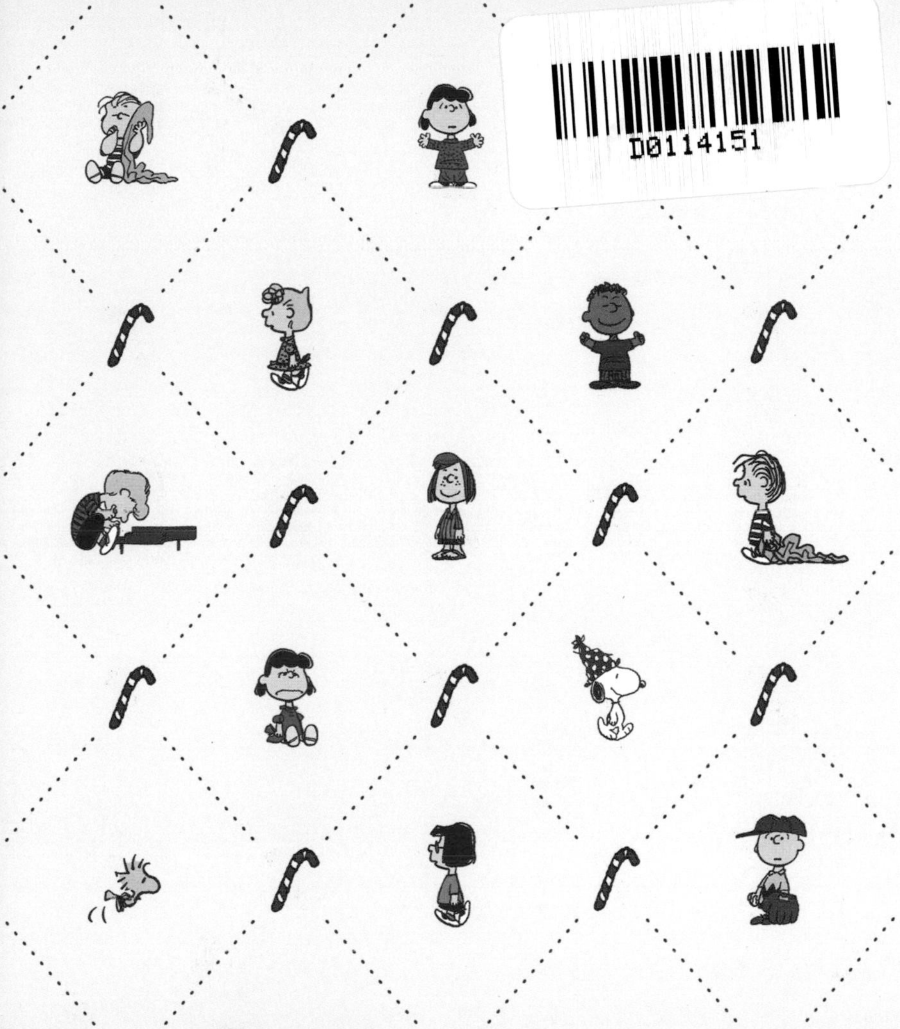

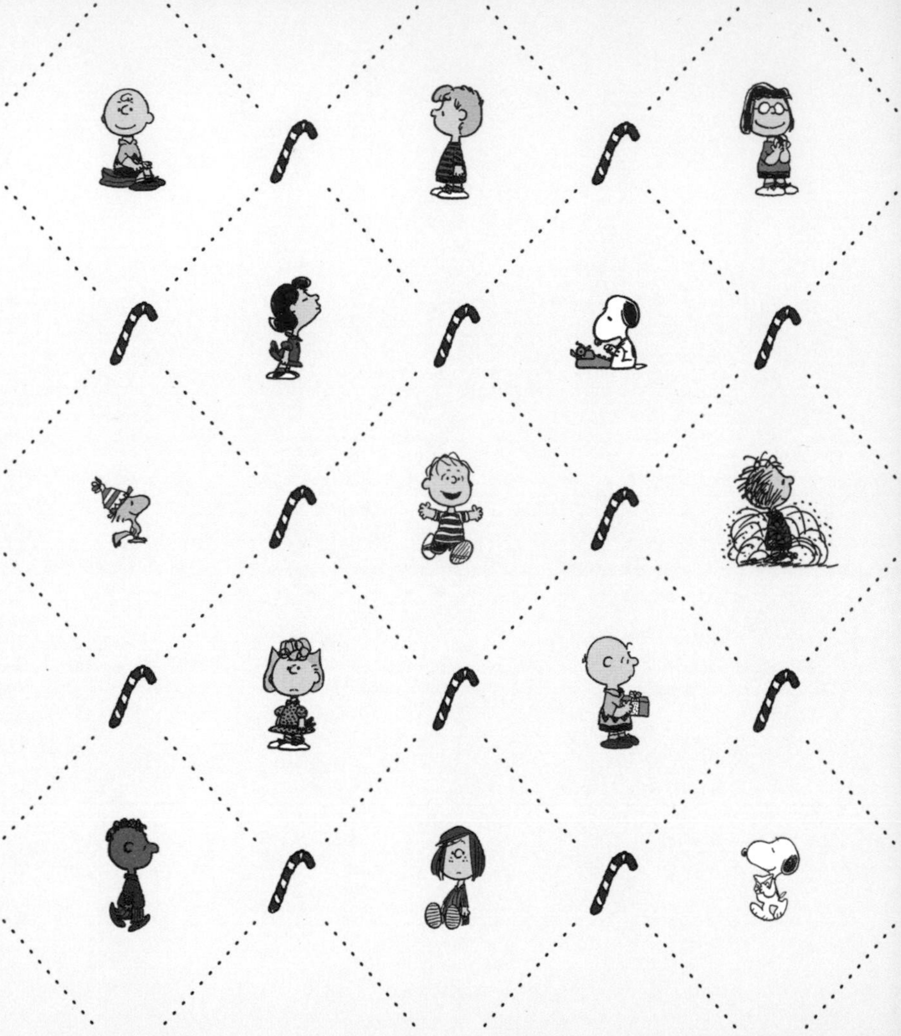

© 2017 by Peanuts Worldwide LLC

Published by Running Press,
An Imprint of Perseus Books, LLC,
A Subsidiary of Hachette Book Group, Inc.

Printed in China

Books published by Running Press are available at special discounts for bulk purchases
in the United States by corporations, institutions, and other organizations.
For more information, please contact the Special Markets Department at Perseus Books,
2300 Chestnut Street, Suite 200, Philadelphia, PA 19103, or call (800) 810-4145,
ext. 5000, or e-mail special.markets@perseusbooks.com.

ISBN 978-0-7624-9149-0
Library of Congress Control Number: 2017936959

9   8   7   6   5   4   3   2   1
Digit on the right indicates the number of this printing

PEANUTS written and drawn by Charles M. Schulz
Design: Rafaela Romaya
Layout: Stuart Polson
Typography: Rockwell and Trend Sans

Running Press Book Publishers
2300 Chestnut Street
Philadelphia, PA 19103-4371

Visit us on the web!
www.runningpress.com
www.snoopy.com

CHARLES M. SCHULZ

# THE PEANUTS GUIDE TO
# CHRISTMAS

RUNNING PRESS
PHILADELPHIA

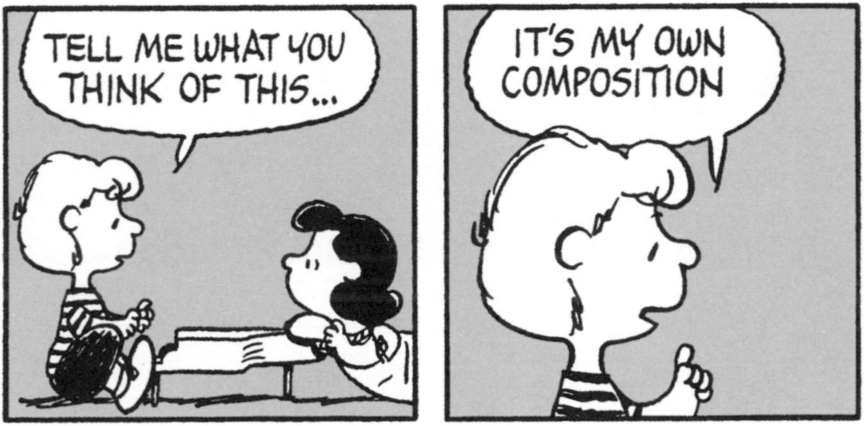
TELL ME WHAT YOU THINK OF THIS...
IT'S MY OWN COMPOSITION

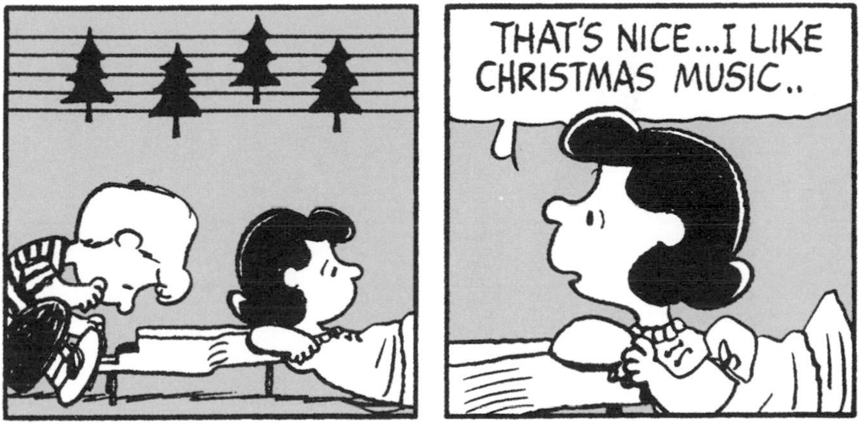
THAT'S NICE...I LIKE CHRISTMAS MUSIC..

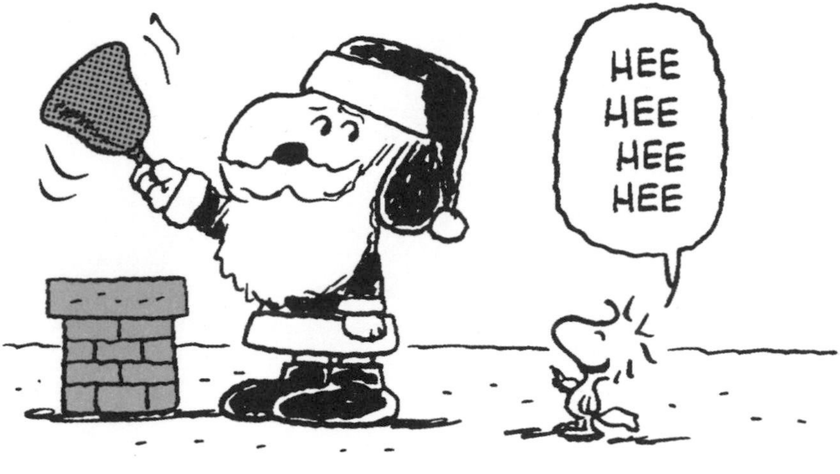
HEE HEE HEE HEE

# CHRISTMAS DECORATIONS SEEM TO GO UP EARLIER EVERY YEAR

I'M MAKING OUT MY CHRISTMAS LIST..
HOW DO YOU SPELL YOUR NAME?

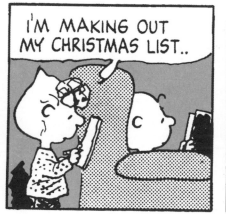

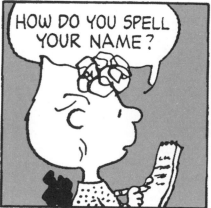

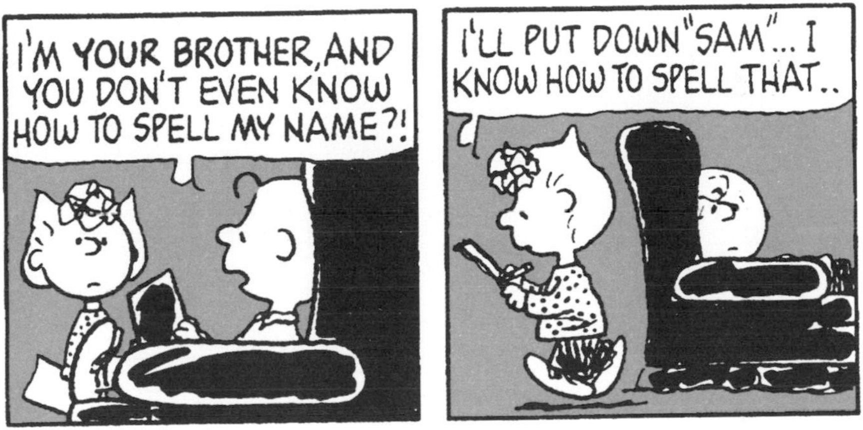
I'M YOUR BROTHER, AND YOU DON'T EVEN KNOW HOW TO SPELL MY NAME?!
I'LL PUT DOWN "SAM"... I KNOW HOW TO SPELL THAT..

THIS IS THE HOLIDAY SEASON
IF YOU WERE SMART, YOU'D WRITE A NICE CHRISTMAS STORY...

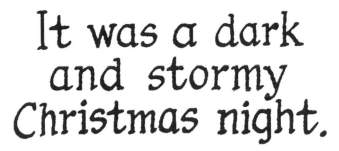

It was a dark
and stormy
Christmas night.

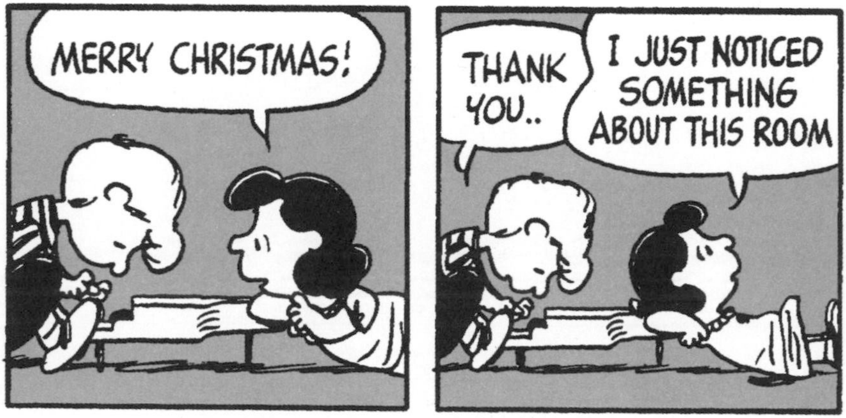
MERRY CHRISTMAS!
THANK YOU..
I JUST NOTICED SOMETHING ABOUT THIS ROOM

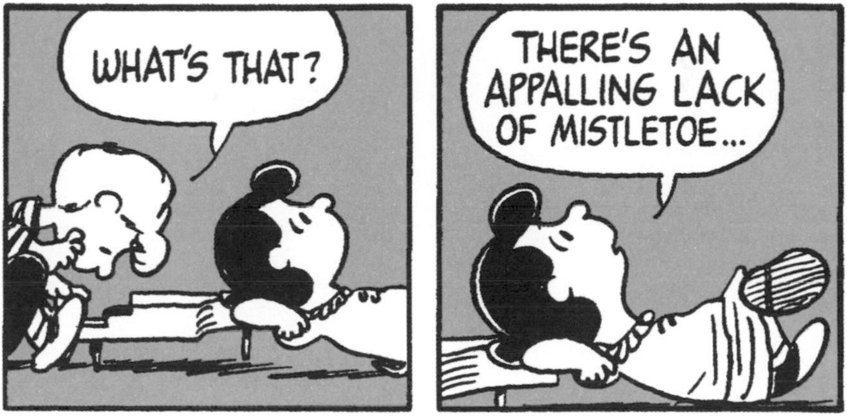
WHAT'S THAT?
THERE'S AN APPALLING LACK OF MISTLETOE...

# EVERYONE SHOULD HAVE A CHRISTMAS TREE

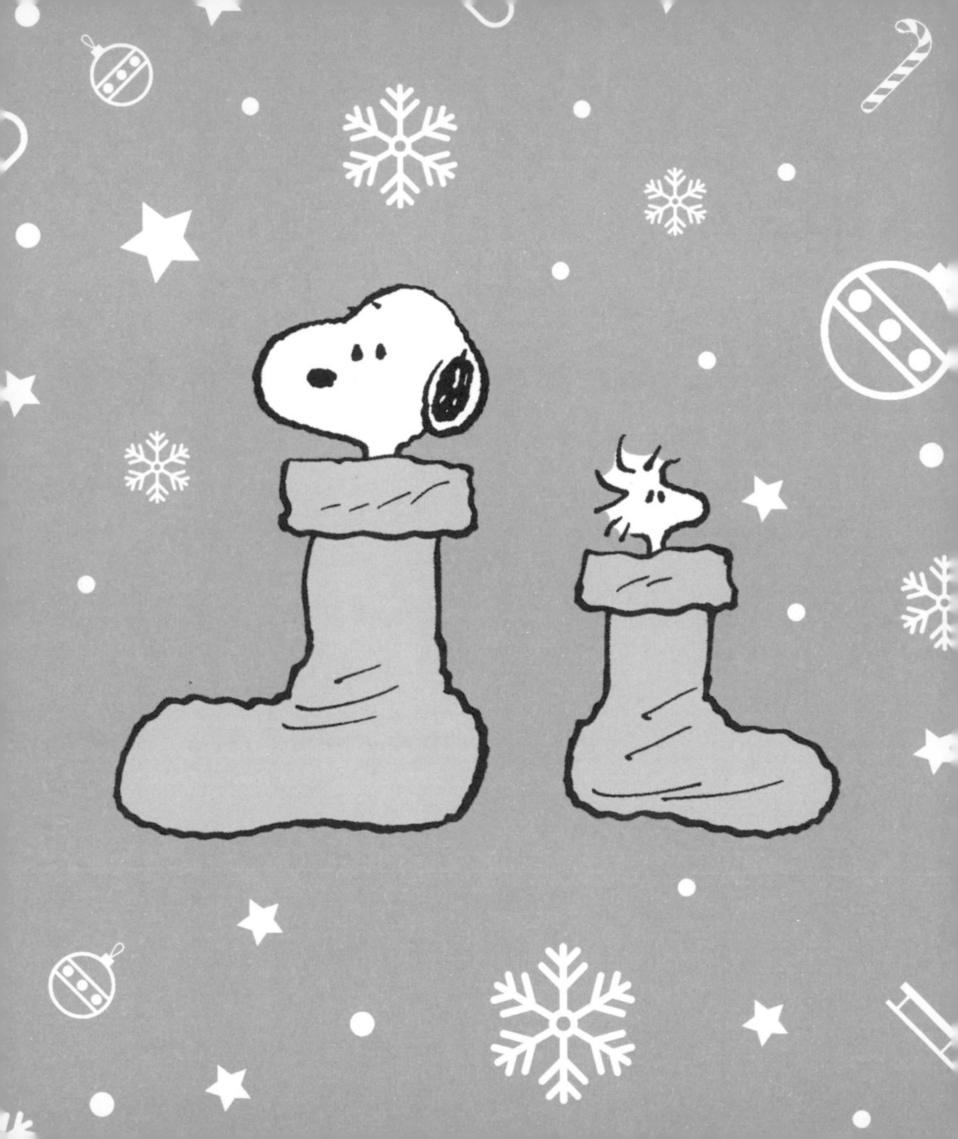

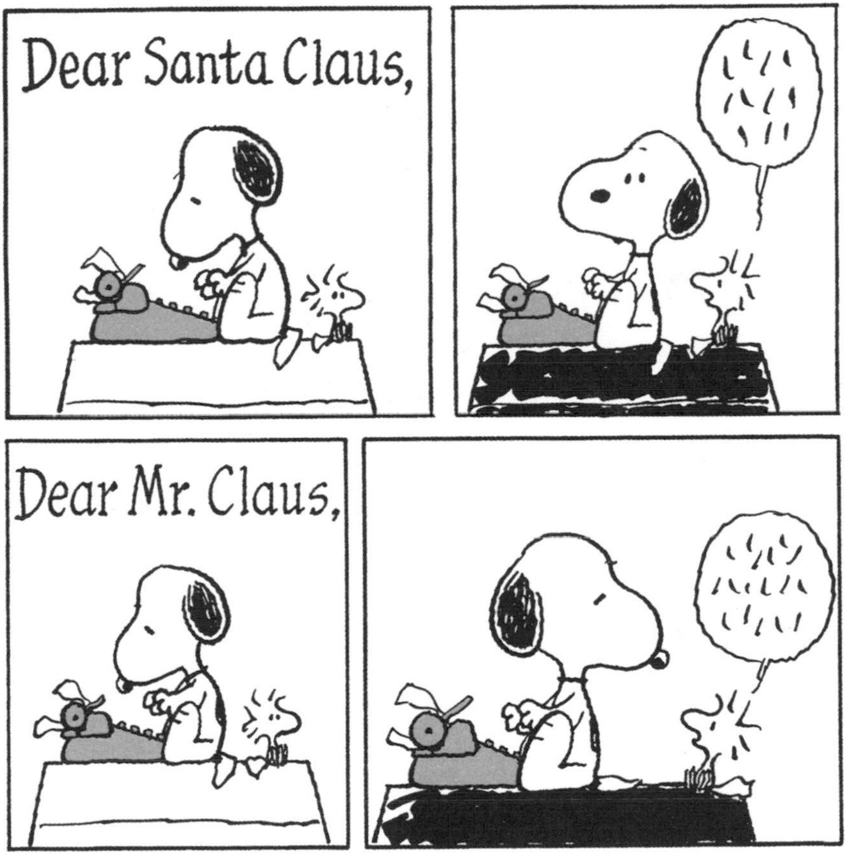

Dear Santa Claus,
Dear Mr. Claus,

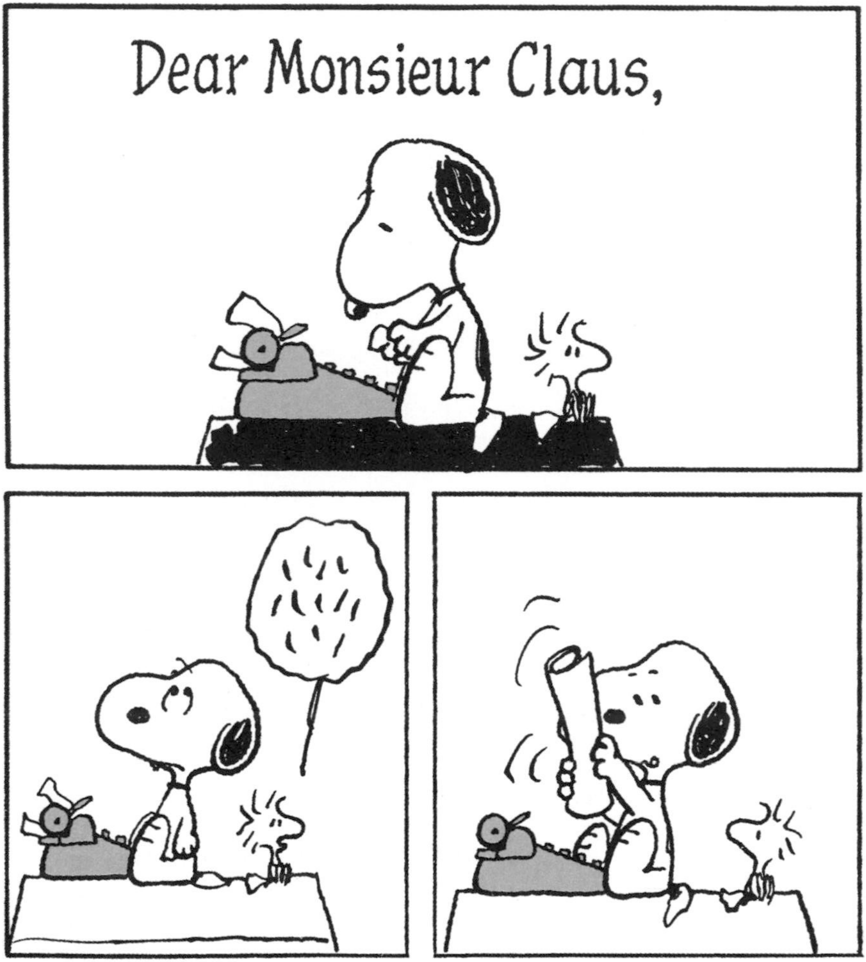
Dear Monsieur Claus,

# Dear Santa Claus,

IT'S VERY EASY TO NEGLECT WRITING LETTERS OF APPRECIATION
THIS IS A GOOD TIME OF YEAR TO WRITE AND TELL SOMEONE HOW MUCH THEY HAVE REALLY MEANT TO YOU...

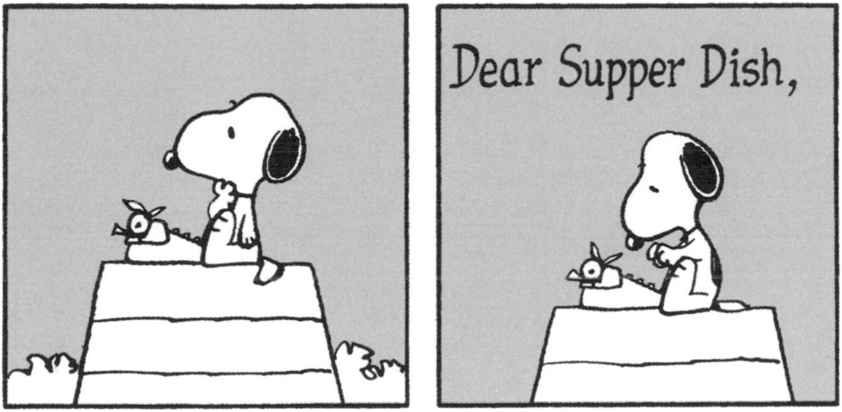
Dear Supper Dish,

# NEVER FALL IN LOVE WITH A SNOWFLAKE

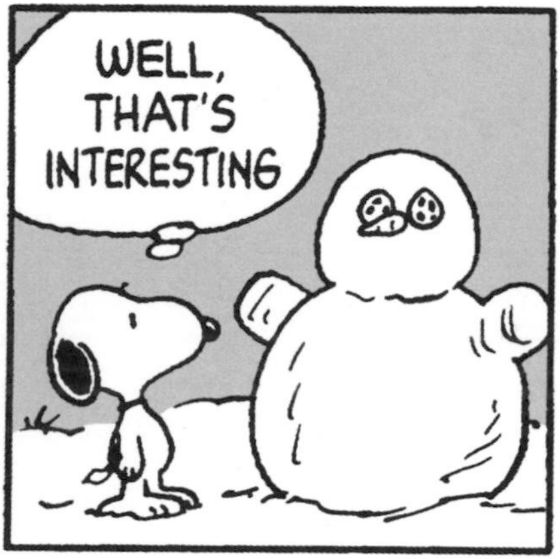
WELL, THAT'S INTERESTING

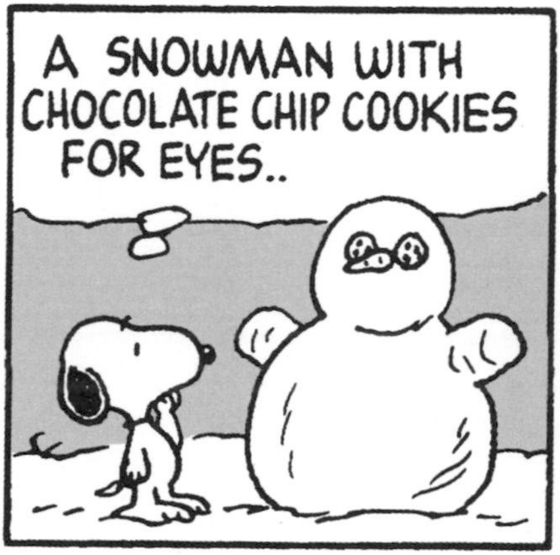
A SNOWMAN WITH CHOCOLATE CHIP COOKIES FOR EYES..

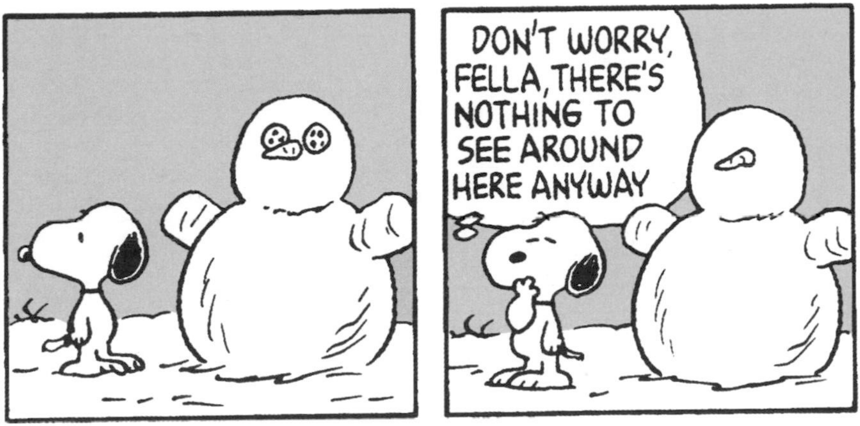
DON'T WORRY, FELLA, THERE'S NOTHING TO SEE AROUND HERE ANYWAY

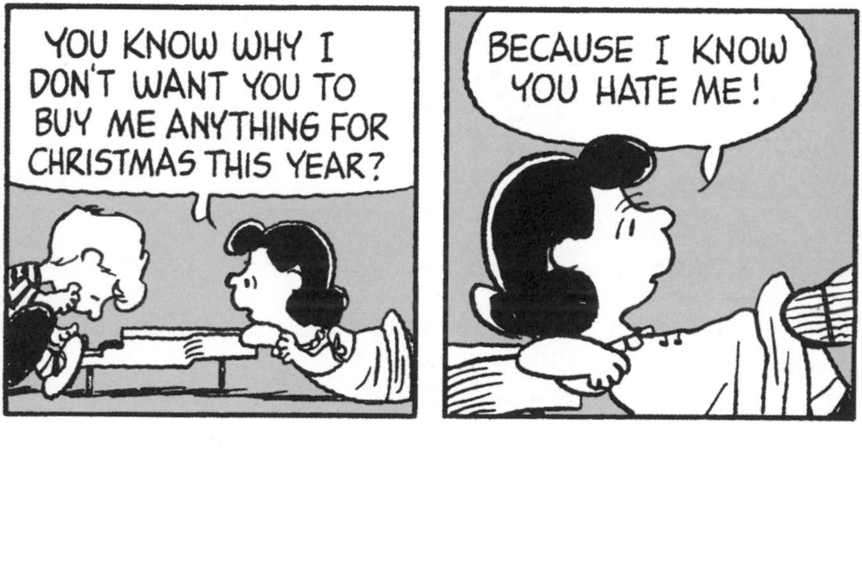
YOU KNOW WHY I DON'T WANT YOU TO BUY ME ANYTHING FOR CHRISTMAS THIS YEAR?
BECAUSE I KNOW YOU HATE ME!

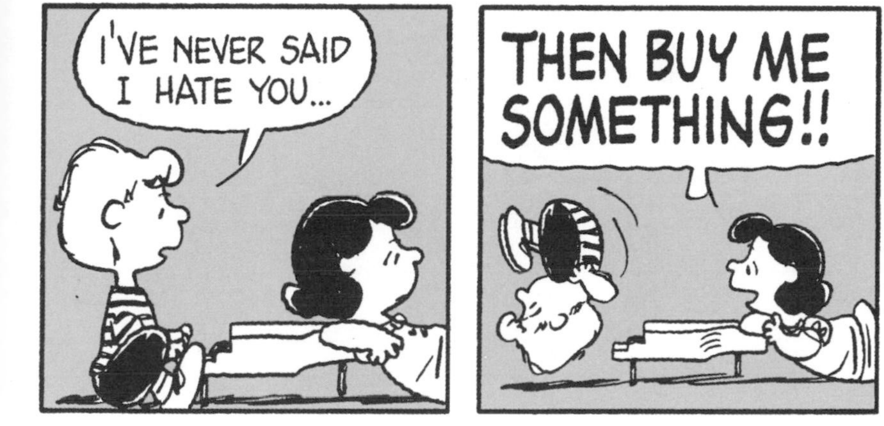

I'VE NEVER SAID I HATE YOU...
THEN BUY ME SOMETHING!!

ONE OF THE GREAT JOYS IN LIFE IS SLIDING ON AN ICY SIDEWALK

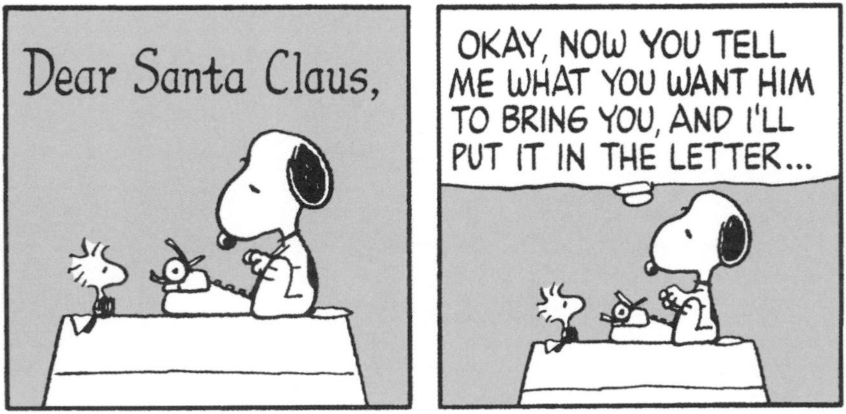

Dear Santa Claus,
OKAY, NOW YOU TELL ME WHAT YOU WANT HIM TO BRING YOU, AND I'LL PUT IT IN THE LETTER...

WHAT COLOR?

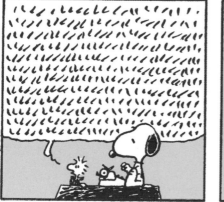

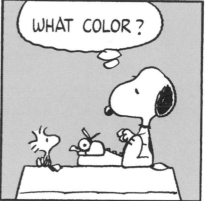

LOOK WHAT I GOT YOU FOR CHRISTMAS..A BOWL FULL OF CHOCOLATE CHIP COOKIES!
WOW!

I JUST HOPE YOU DON'T EAT 'EM ALL AT ONCE..
WHAT DID HE SAY?

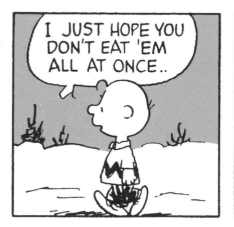

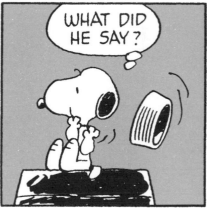

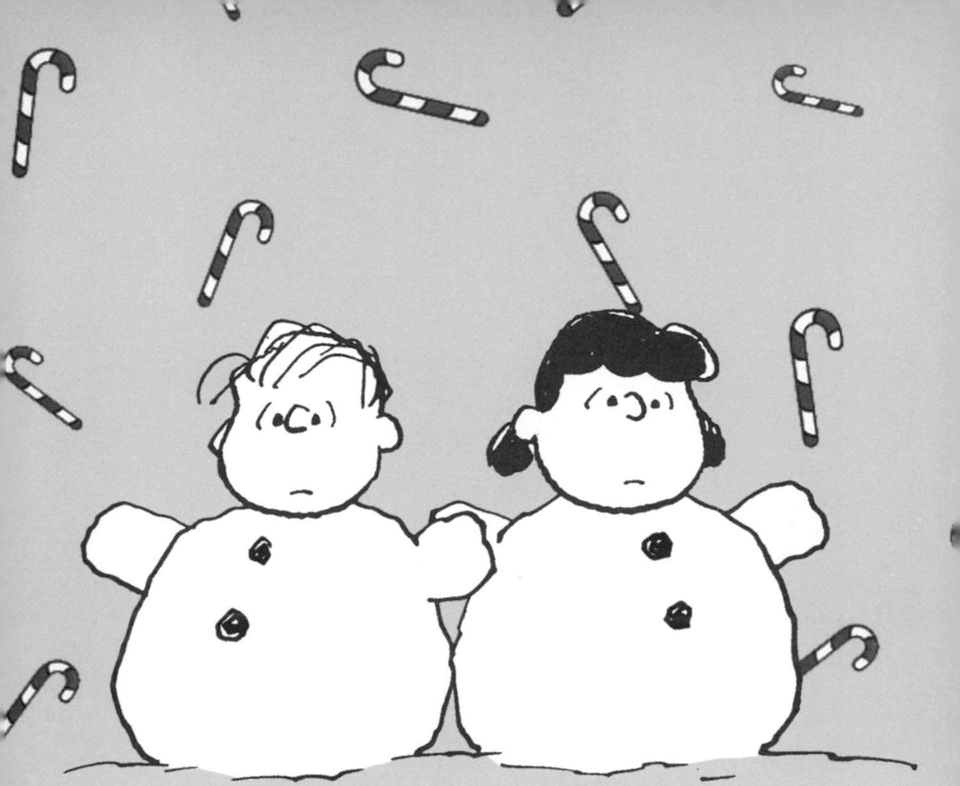

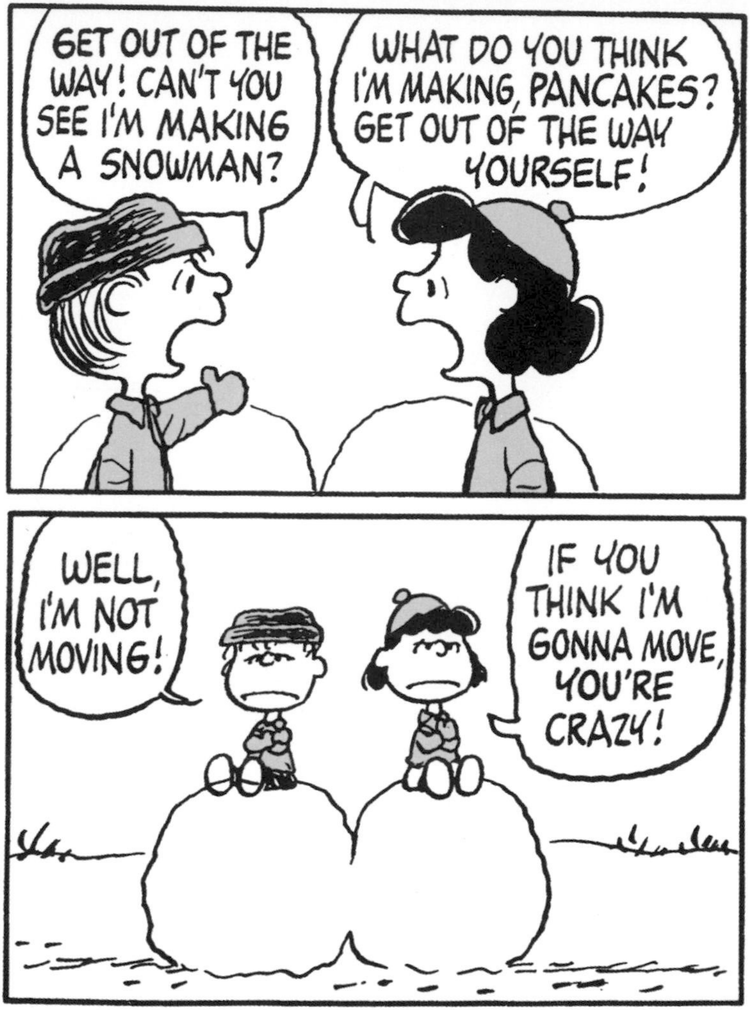
GET OUT OF THE WAY! CAN'T YOU SEE I'M MAKING A SNOWMAN?
WHAT DO YOU THINK I'M MAKING, PANCAKES? GET OUT OF THE WAY YOURSELF!
WELL, I'M NOT MOVING!
IF YOU THINK I'M GONNA MOVE, YOU'RE CRAZY!

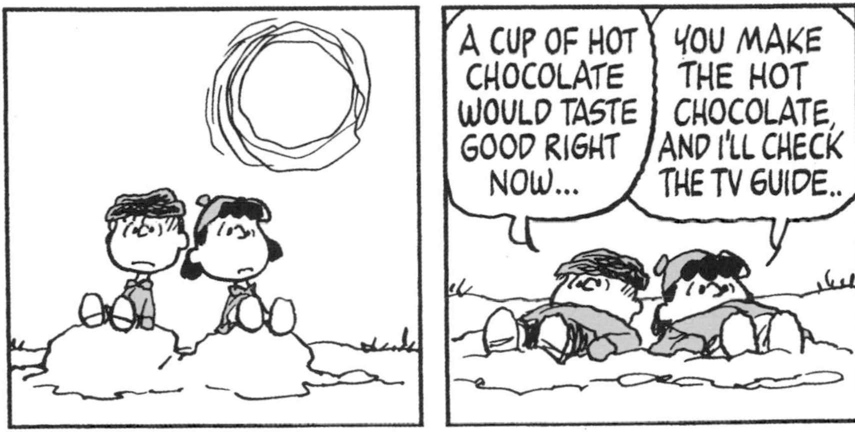
A CUP OF HOT CHOCOLATE WOULD TASTE GOOD RIGHT NOW...
YOU MAKE THE HOT CHOCOLATE, AND I'LL CHECK THE TV GUIDE..

HE HAS THESE REINDEER, SEE, AND THEY FLY THROUGH THE AIR PULLING HIS SLED...
AND IF YOU BELIEVE THAT, I HAVE A GOLD BIRD NEST THAT I'LL SELL YOU FOR A DOLLAR!

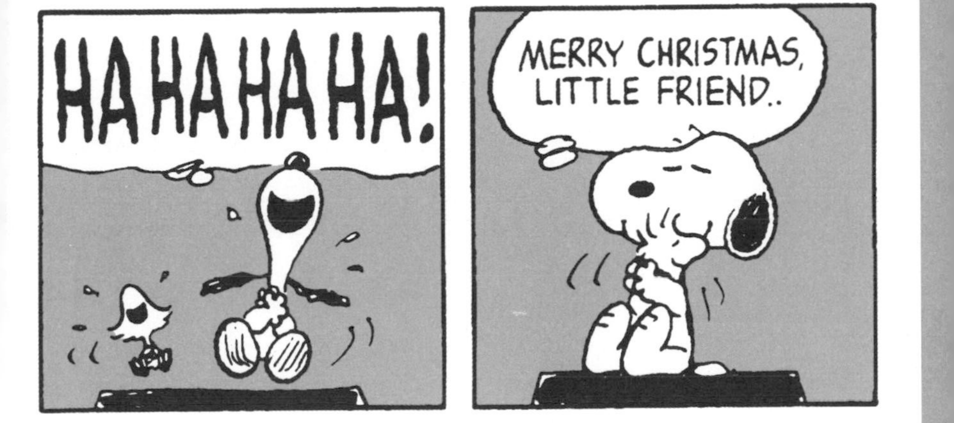
HA HA HA HA HA!
MERRY CHRISTMAS, LITTLE FRIEND..

THERE WERE THREE WISE MEN, SEE...
THEY CAME FROM THE EAST, AND THEY WERE LOOKING FOR BETHLEHEM

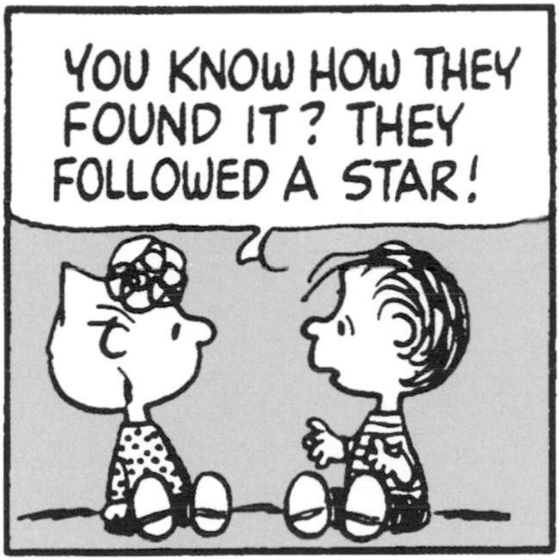
YOU KNOW HOW THEY FOUND IT? THEY FOLLOWED A STAR!
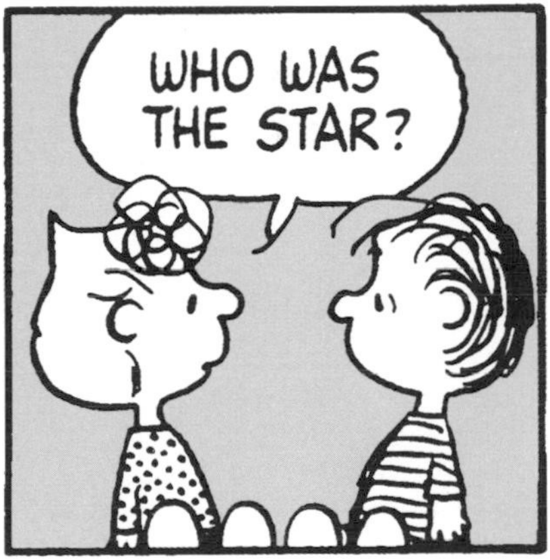
WHO WAS THE STAR?

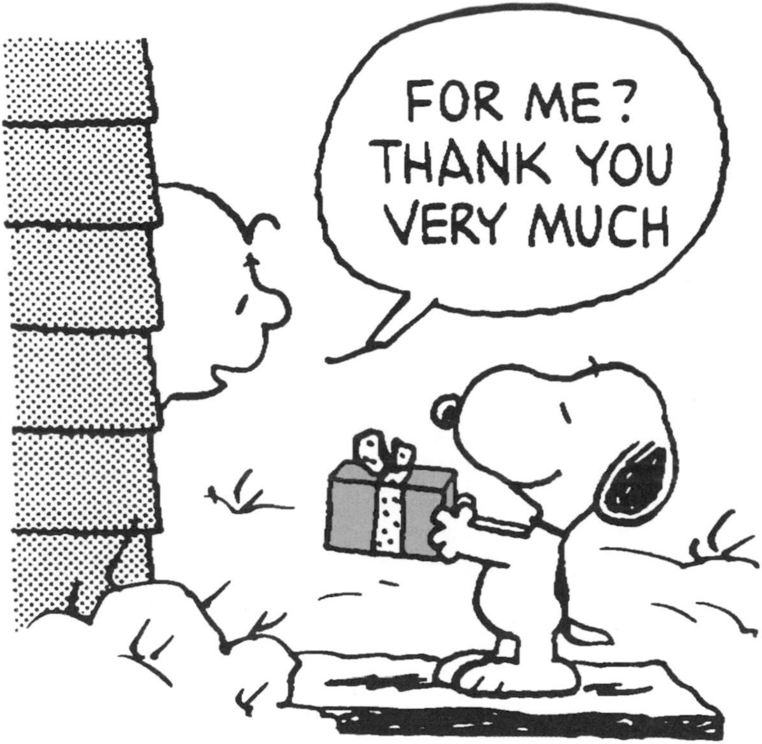
FOR ME? THANK YOU VERY MUCH

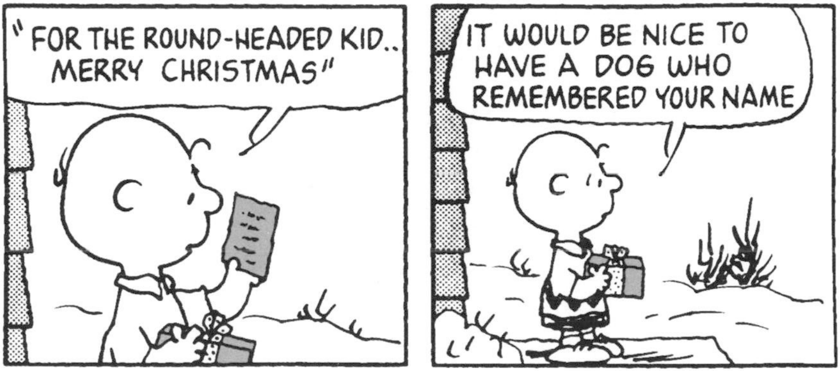
"FOR THE ROUND-HEADED KID.. MERRY CHRISTMAS"
IT WOULD BE NICE TO HAVE A DOG WHO REMEMBERED YOUR NAME

# THE ONLY WAY TO BEAT THE COLD WEATHER IS TO HIBERNATE

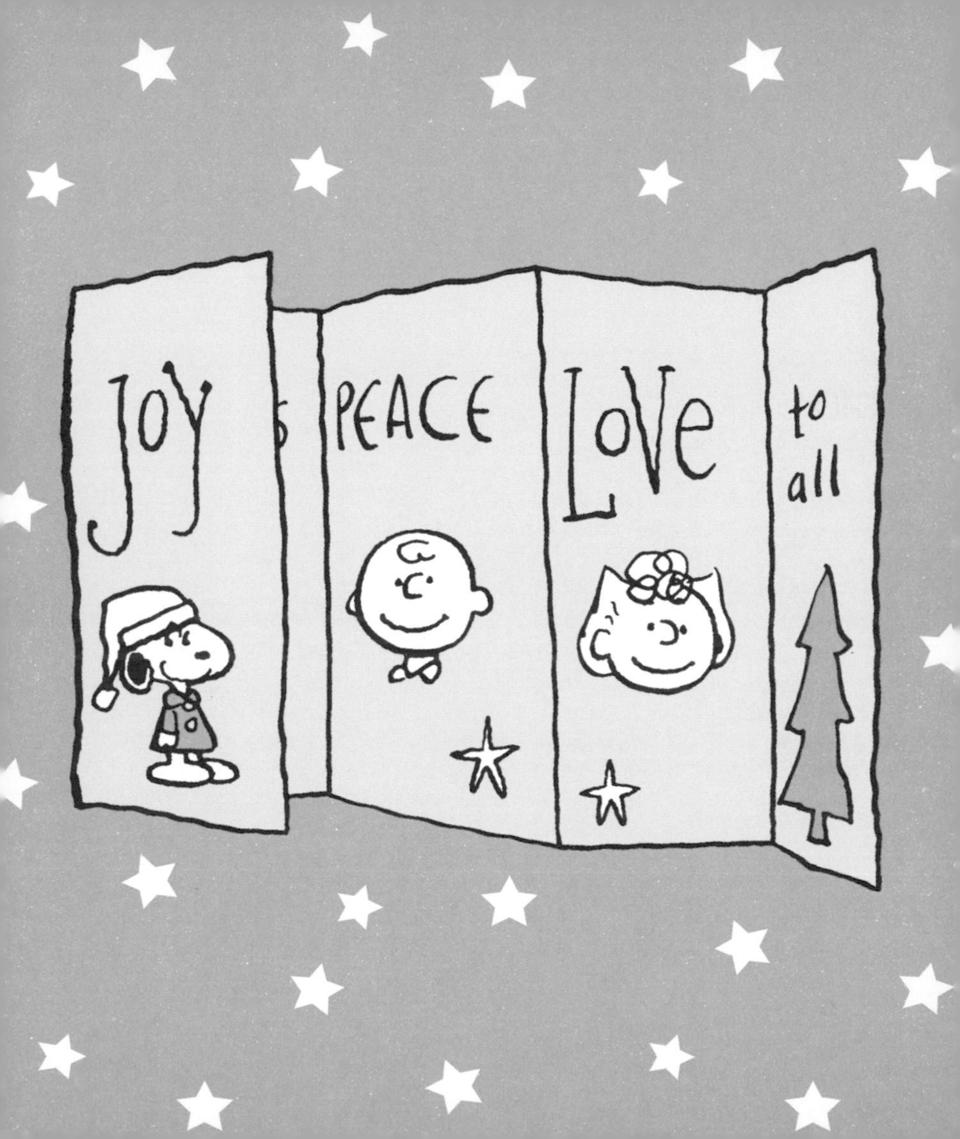
JOY
PEACE
LOVE
to all

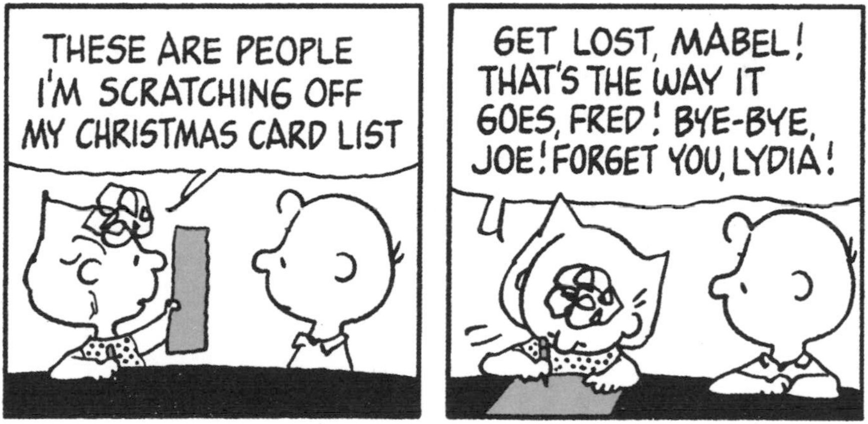
THESE ARE PEOPLE I'M SCRATCHING OFF MY CHRISTMAS CARD LIST
GET LOST, MABEL! THAT'S THE WAY IT GOES, FRED! BYE-BYE, JOE! FORGET YOU, LYDIA!

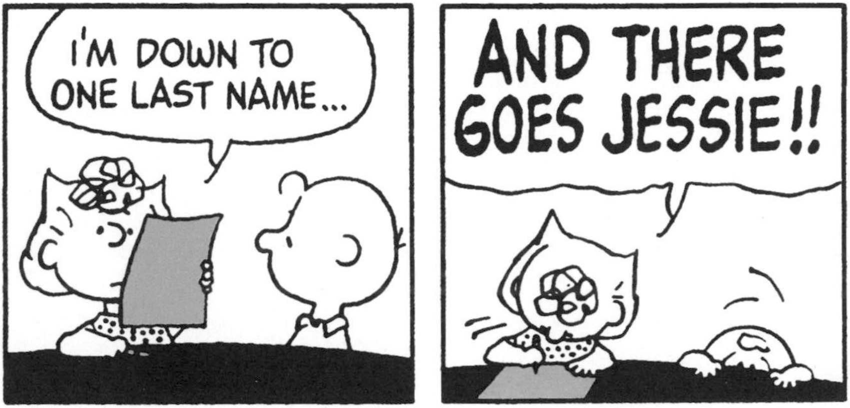
I'M DOWN TO ONE LAST NAME...
AND THERE GOES JESSIE!!

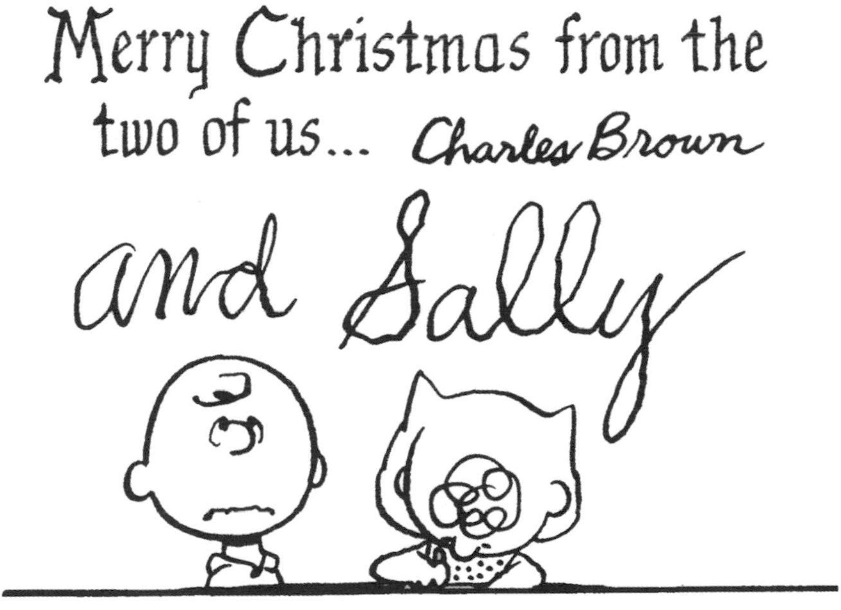
Merry Christmas from the two of us... Charles Brown
and Sally

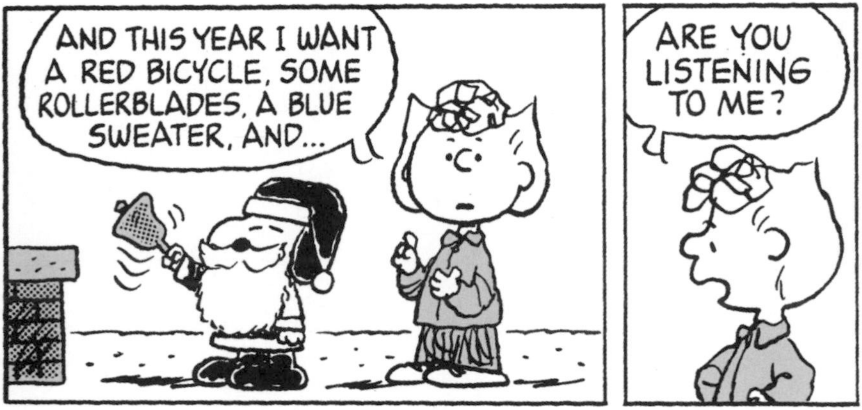
AND THIS YEAR I WANT A RED BICYCLE, SOME ROLLERBLADES, A BLUE SWEATER, AND...
ARE YOU LISTENING TO ME?

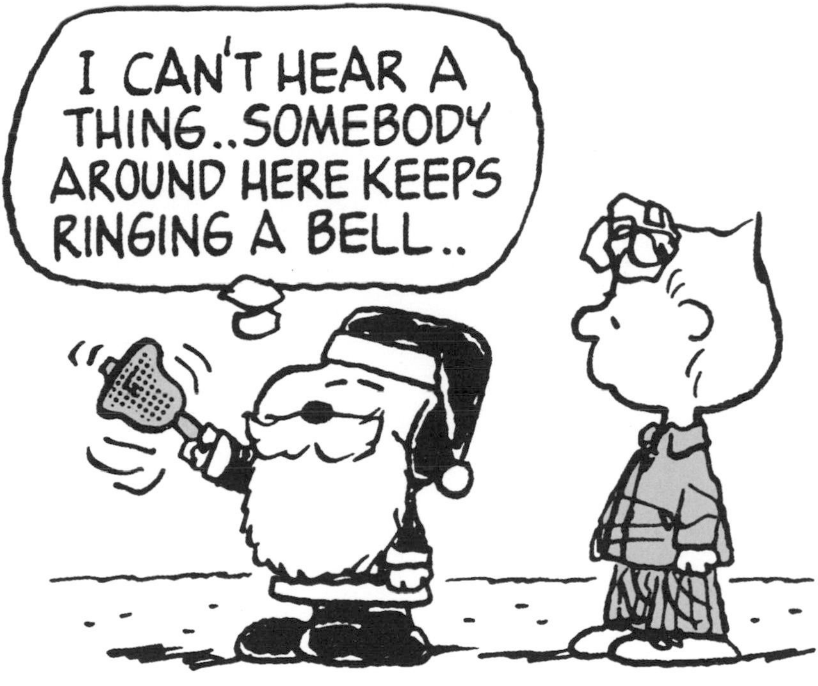
I CAN'T HEAR A THING..SOMEBODY AROUND HERE KEEPS RINGING A BELL..

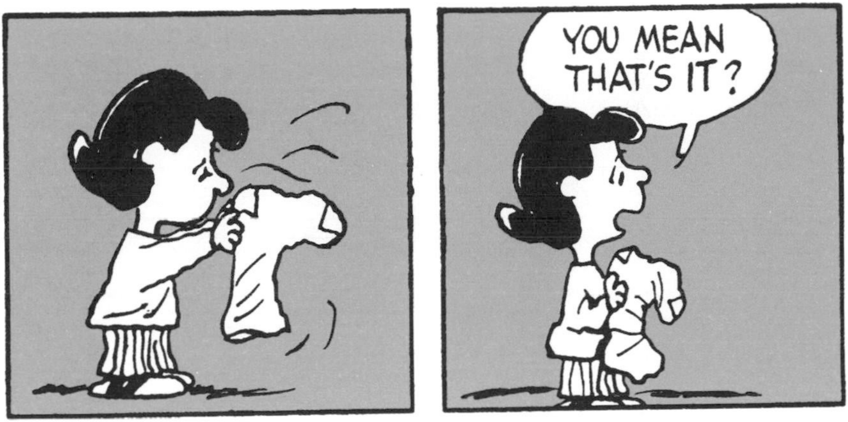
YOU MEAN THAT'S IT?

ONE OF THE
GREAT JOYS
IN LIFE IS
CUTTING DOWN
YOUR OWN
CHRISTMAS TREE

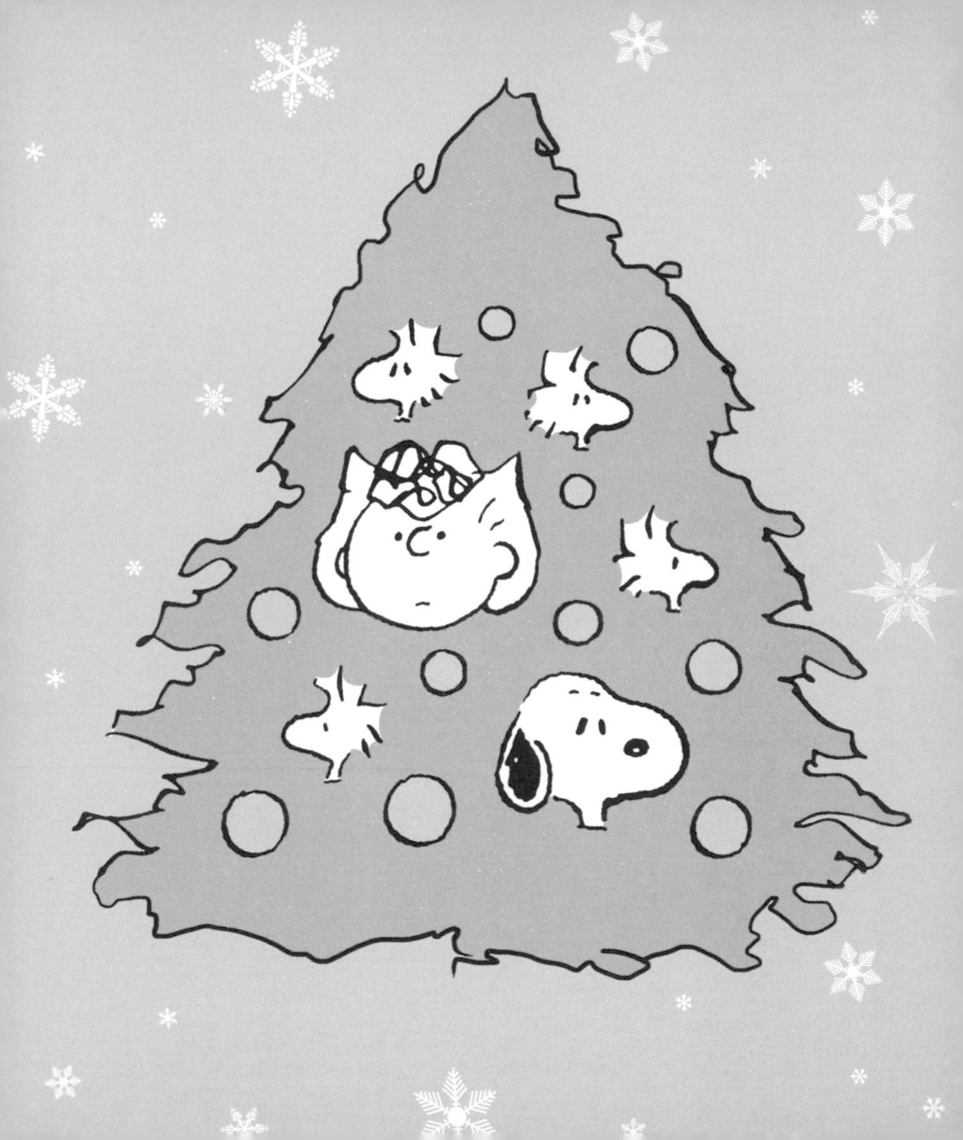

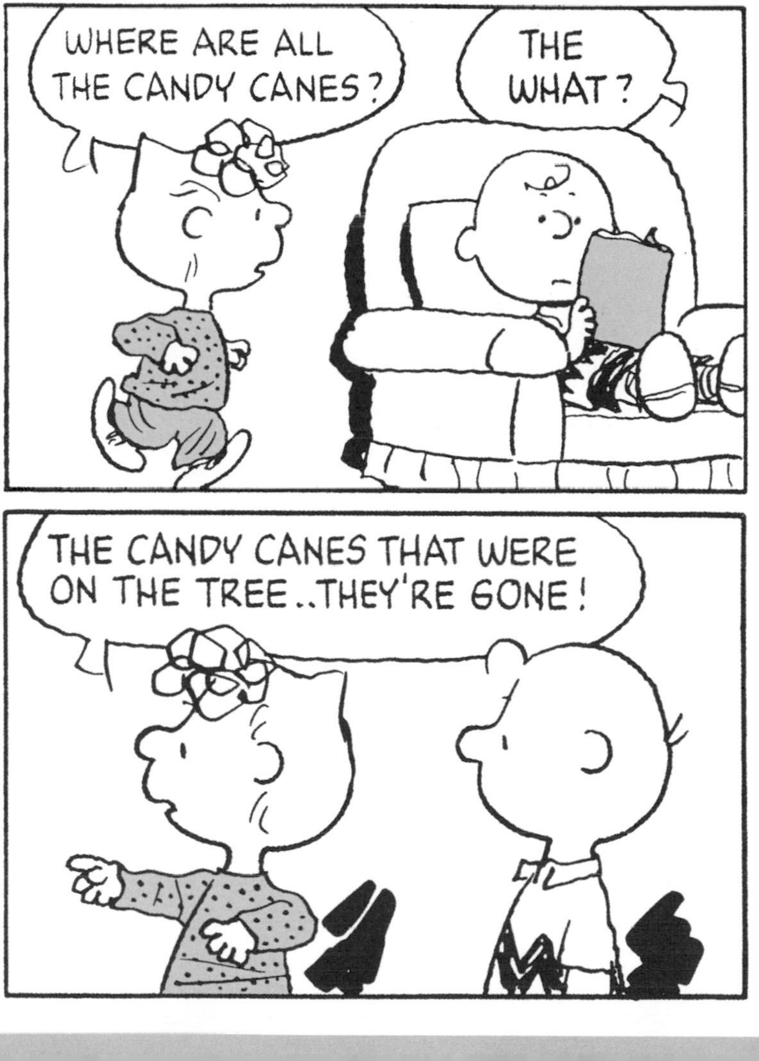
WHERE ARE ALL THE CANDY CANES?
THE WHAT?
THE CANDY CANES THAT WERE ON THE TREE..THEY'RE GONE!

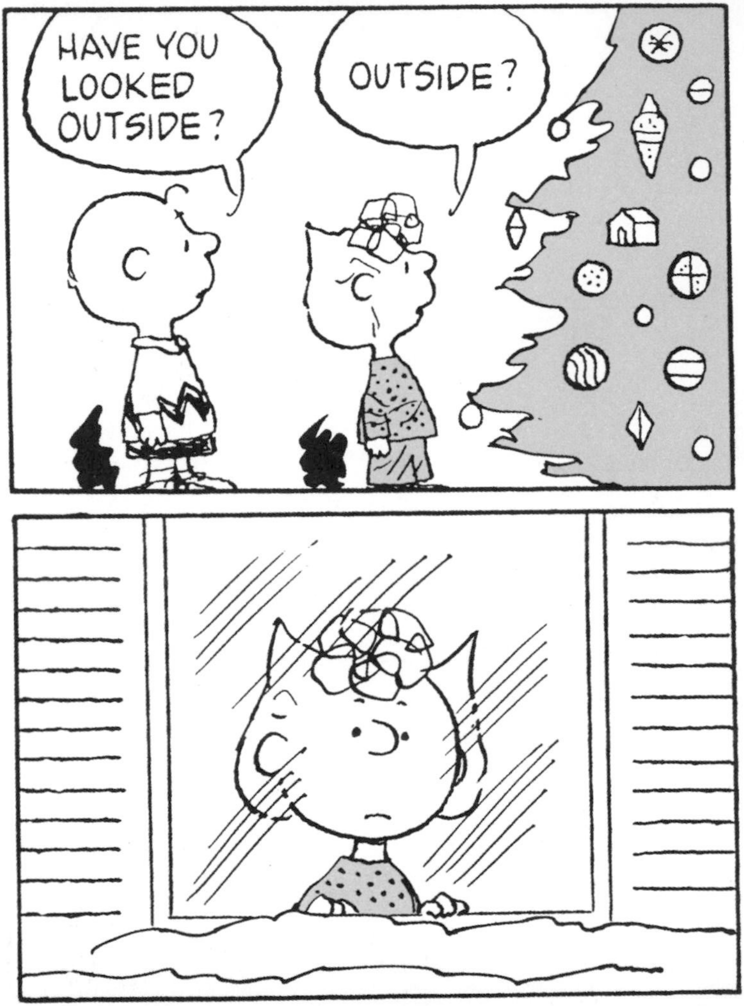
HAVE YOU LOOKED OUTSIDE?
OUTSIDE?

# HAPPINESS IS CATCHING SNOWFLAKES ON YOUR TONGUE

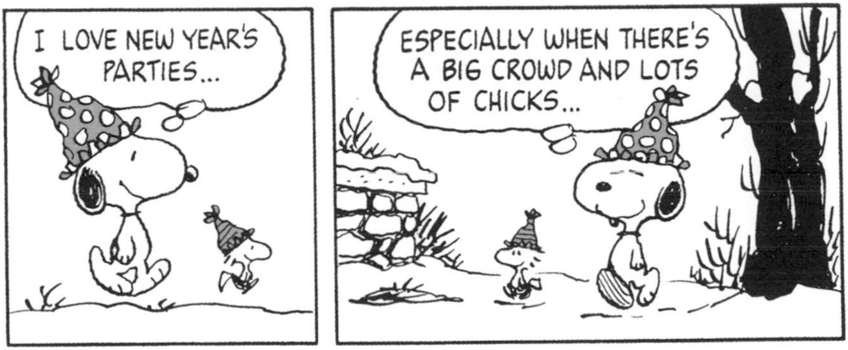
I LOVE NEW YEAR'S PARTIES...
ESPECIALLY WHEN THERE'S A BIG CROWD AND LOTS OF CHICKS...

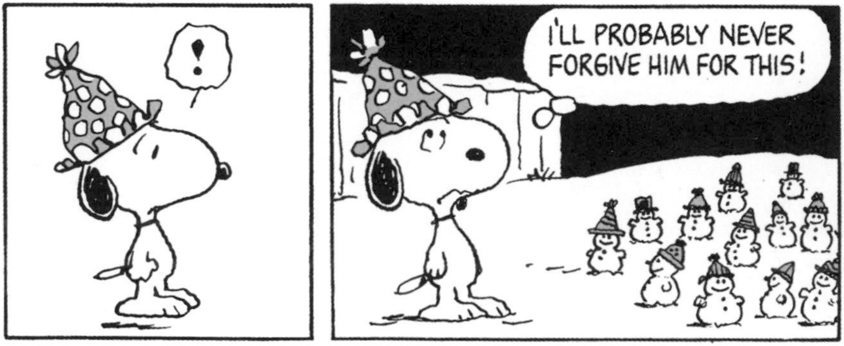
!
I'LL PROBABLY NEVER FORGIVE HIM FOR THIS!

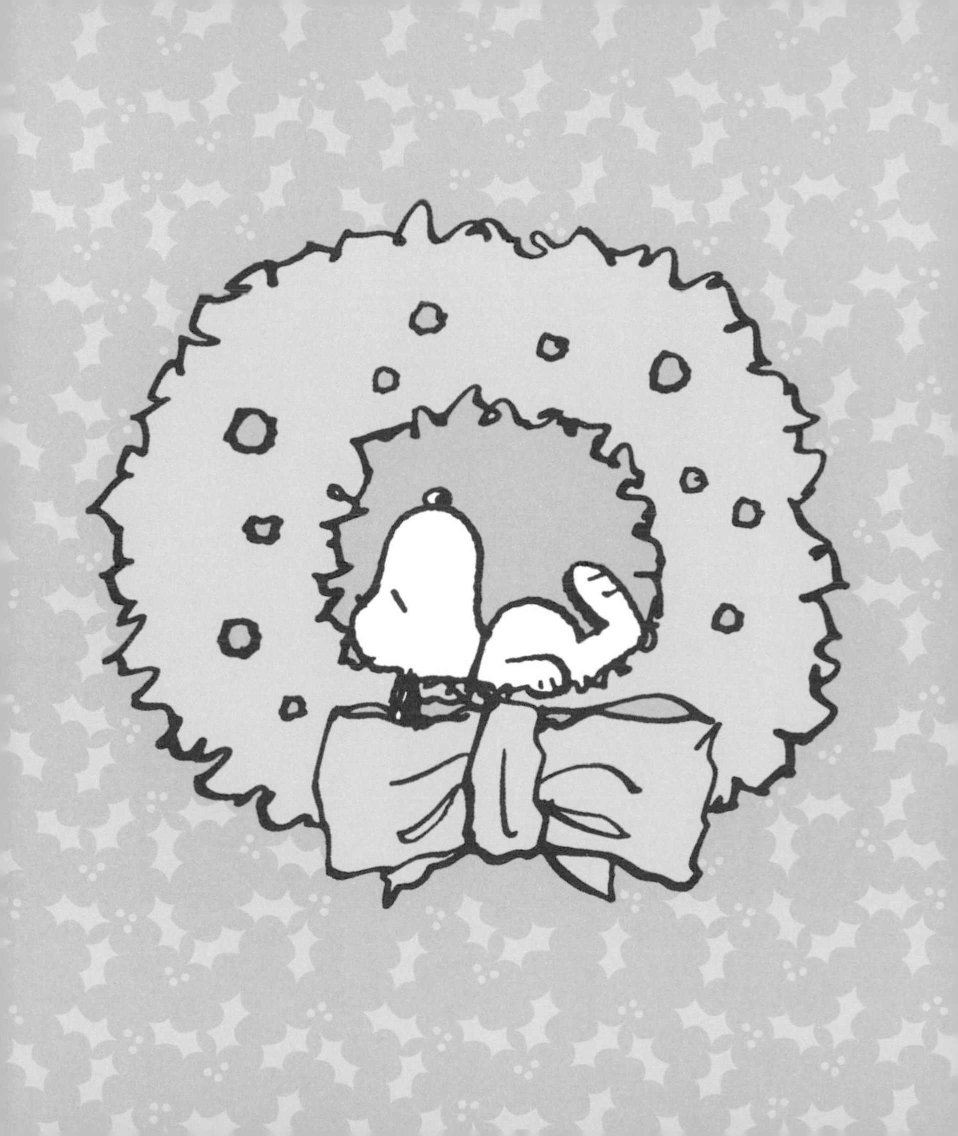

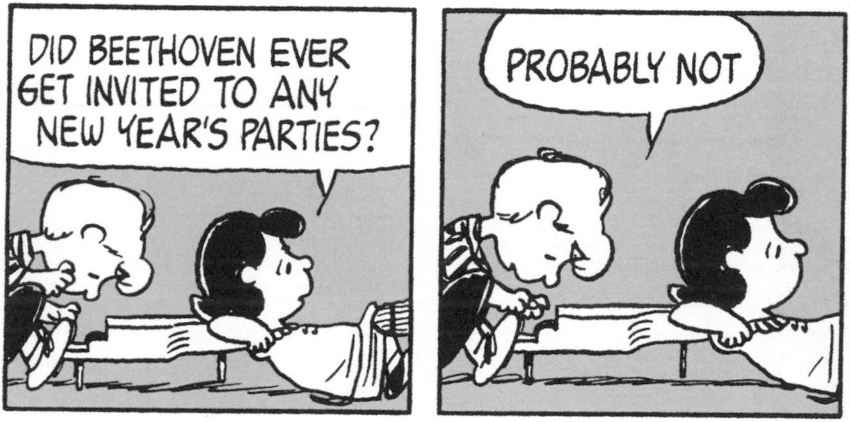
DID BEETHOVEN EVER GET INVITED TO ANY NEW YEAR'S PARTIES?
PROBABLY NOT

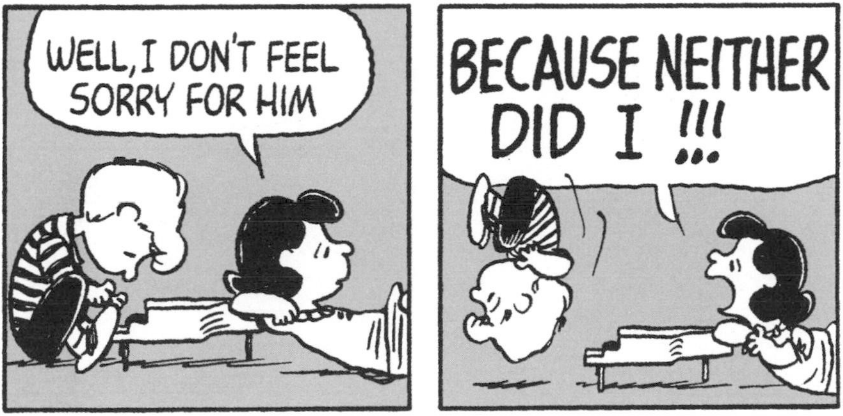
WELL, I DON'T FEEL SORRY FOR HIM
BECAUSE NEITHER DID I !!!

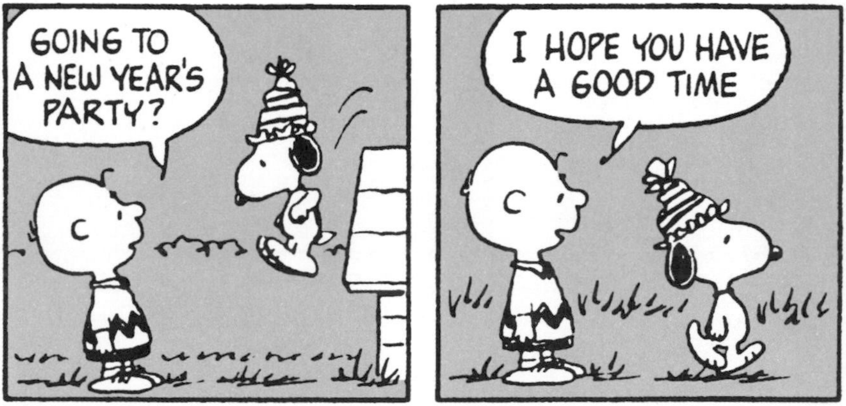
GOING TO A NEW YEAR'S PARTY?
I HOPE YOU HAVE A GOOD TIME

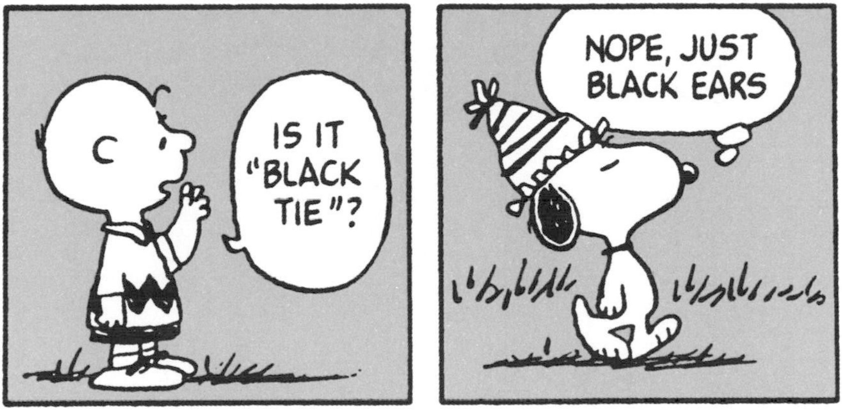
IS IT "BLACK TIE"?
NOPE, JUST BLACK EARS